THE SCULPTED VEGAN

44 HIGH PROTEIN VEGAN RECIPES

FOR SCULPTING MUSCLE AND BURNING FAT

KIM CONSTABLE

CONTENTS

INTRODUCTION 6

BREAKFASTS
BAKED VEGGIE PAN OMELETTE 11
BREAKFAST BURRITO 12
COCONUT CREAM PROTEIN SHAKE 13
OVERNIGHT BIRCHER WITH BLUEBERRIES 14
SUPER PROTEIN SMOOTHIE 15
SUPER SIMPLE PROTEIN OATMEAL 16
ULTIMATE SUPER PROTEIN BREAKFAST 17
TOFU SCRAMBLE WITH CHILI, CORIANDER & GARLIC (UNDER 10 MINUTES TO PREPARE) 19

BURGERS
CANNELLINI BEAN PATTIES 22
CHICKPEA BURGERS 23
SPICY TOFU & MUSHROOM BURGER 24
VEGAN SLOPPY JOES 25
TOFU BURGERS (WITH CRUSHED TOMATO SALSA AND CREAMY BASIL DRESSING) 27

MAINS
CHILLI TOFU STIR-FRY 30
CRUSHED PUY LENTILS WITH TAHINI AND CUMIN 31
ITALIAN NO-MEATBALLS 32
SMOKY BUTTERNUT SQUASH AND BEAN CASSEROLE, WITH TOMATO SALSA 33
SPICED CAULIFLOWER & CHICKPEA CURRY 34
THAI PEANUT TOFU WITH MIX VEG BOWL 35
THE BEST VEGAN MEDITERRANEAN QUICHE IN THE WORLD 36
VEGAN MEXICAN CHILLI 37
VEGAN MOUSSAKA 39

SALADS

- BEANSPROUT & MANGO SALAD WITH AGAVE CASHEWS 42
- CARROT AND MUNG BEAN SALAD 43
- SPINACH, PEACH AND PECAN SALAD 44
- CITRUS TOFU SALAD WITH AVOCADO 45
- MANGO AND CURRIED CHICKPEA SALAD 46
- MUSHROOM MELT WITH GREEN SALAD 47
- CAULIFLOWER BITES & MEXICAN STREET SALAD 49

SLOW COOKER

- SLOW COOKER BALSAMIC TOFU 52
- SLOW COOKER BEAN & SPINACH GOULASH 53
- SLOW COOKER JAMAICAN TOFU & BEAN STEW 54
- SLOW COOKER NEW MEXICO GREEN CHILLI BEAN & TOFU STEW 55
- SLOW COOKER TOFU BEAN CASSEROLE 57

SNACKS

- APPLE RINGS 60
- ULTIMATE PROTEIN FLAPJACKS 61
- CARROT CAKE GRANOLA BARS 62
- CHOCOLATE PROTEIN TRUFFLES 63
- MANGO, LIME & COCONUT FROZEN YOGHURT 64
- STRAWBERRY PARFAIT 65

SOUPS

- BLENDED BROCCOLI SOUP 68
- CURRIED RED LENTIL SOUP 69
- MINESTRONE SOUP 70
- SUPER GREENS & BEAN SOUP 71

INTRODUCTION

44 HIGH PROTEIN VEGAN RECIPES FOR SCULPTING MUSCLE AND BURNING FAT

"I have cooked and created the best high plant-protein cuisine, specifically for vegan athletes, that exists in the industry. And it's all here in an easy to follow recipe book."
Kim Constable

I have always been a fanatical cook. My mother suffers from the overfeeding gene, which I guess I inherited by default. I love nothing more than gathering people together for lunches, dinners and kitchen suppers, serving multiple dishes of delicious food. When I became vegan, my family and friends gave a collective gasp of horror. What would happen to my notorious dinner parties where we gathered around the kitchen table, eating and drinking into the "wee small hours" (as we say in Belfast, where I'm from)?

However, I was determined that being vegan wasn't going to cramp my style. If anything, I was out to prove to the world that you don't need to eat animals to enjoy delicious food. I set about "veganising" my favourite meals, testing and tweaking until they were so perfect, that not even the most hardened carnivore could complain. I experimented with making my own cheeses, tofu and nut milks, roping in my friends and family to critique my creations and opening their minds to new possibilities that didn't harm animals.

When I started body-building, it was a no brainer to continue my vegan journey. My diet now called for me to measure my macros (protein, carbohydrate and fat) and I was pleased to discover that my daily meals contained more than enough protein for my muscle building needs. And if they didn't, all I needed to do was add a scoop of protein powder here, or a few extra flaxseeds there, and hey presto, I hit my target.

So when people started asking me "How do you get your protein?" I was confused. Surely they knew that protein is contained in nearly every single whole food? Even spinach contains more than 4g of protein per 100g! But clearly, the world had been so brainwashed into thinking that they needed animal protein to build muscle, they had no idea that it was easy to hit your daily protein needs on a vegan diet.

My decision to compete on stage as a physique athlete had less to do with wanting to prance around in a sparkly bikini with a Nutella-esque tan, and more to do with busting the myths that surround muscle and protein. When you compete as an athlete at the highest level in your sport, people sit up and take notice. When you do it as a vegan, people start to believe that it's possible.

This book contains some of my favourite recipes for building muscle and burning fat. They are the exact recipes that I have created and eaten, and that took me all the way to the stage as a vegan physique competitor. And to make it extra easy, we've included the nutrient breakdown of each dish, so you can easily track your own daily nutritional needs. I hope you enjoy these recipes as much as I enjoyed creating them. Feel free to experiment and omit things you don't like and add things you do. And give yourself a high five and a bum slap for the fact that you are not only contributing to your own health and well being, but you're basically saving the planet in the process.

With love
Kim xo

BREAKFASTS

BREAKFASTS

BAKED VEGGIE PAN OMELETTE

SERVES: 4

ROASTED VEGGIES
- 2 tablespoons coconut oil (plus more to re-grease pan)
- 2 large leeks, trimmed and sliced on an angle into 2½ cm pieces
- 2 large carrots, peeled and sliced lengthwise
- 1 large red onion, peeled and sliced into thick half-moons
- 130g green beans, ends trimmed
- 425g cherry tomatoes, sliced in half
- 2 tablespoons fresh rosemary or thyme, or 1 tablespoon dried
- Salt and freshly ground black pepper

OMELETTE
- 425g soft silken tofu
- 150ml unsweetened plain soy milk
- 65g garbanzo/chickpea flour (also called Gram flour)
- 3 tablespoons nutritional yeast
- 2 heaped tablespoons whole-grain mustard
- 1 tablespoon coconut oil
- ½ teaspoon baking powder
- ½ teaspoon ground turmeric
- 1 teaspoon salt
- Generous pinch of kala namak (Indian black salt optional)

DIRECTIONS

Prepare the veggies: Preheat the oven to 175°C/Gas mark 4. Toss together the coconut oil, leeks, carrots, onion, green beans, tomatoes, and herbs in a 20 x 30 x 5cm baking dish. When everything is coated with oil, spread in an even layer in the pan. Sprinkle a little salt and pepper on top.

Roast the veggies for about 30 minutes, stirring occasionally, until golden and tender. Remove the pan from the oven and transfer the vegetables to a dish or cutting board. (This can be done a day in advance and kept in the fridge)

When the baking pan is just cool enough to touch, line with foil (maybe slip on a pair of baking mitts for this part). Generously grease the foil with additional coconut oil.

Make the omelette: In a blender. pulse together until smooth the tofu, soy milk, gram flour, nutritional yeast, coconut oil, mustard, baking powder, turmeric, salt, and kala namak, if using. Pour into the pan and gently shake the pan a few times to remove any air bubbles.

Arrange the roasted vegetables on top of the tofu mixture in a pleasing way. Return the pan to the oven and bake for 20 to 25 minutes, or until the tofu layer is lightly puffed, golden, and no longer liquid but instead a soft, solid texture when poked with a knife.

Remove from the oven and set aside to cool for at least 5 minutes before slicing. Use a spatula to gently remove squares of the omelette from the pan. The tofu will firm up considerably if chilled overnight and reheats well.

Serve with a green salad and some sourdough bread. (Not included in the Nutrition Facts)

Nutrition Facts

Servings: 4

Amount Per Serving	
Calories 299	
	% Daily Value*
Total Fat 15.9g	20%
Saturated Fat 1.9g	10%
Trans Fat 0g	
Cholesterol 0mg	0%
Sodium 1099mg	48%
Potassium 794mg	17%
Total Carb 22.3g	7%
Dietary Fiber 8.1g	29%
Sugars 6.7g	
Protein 19.6g	
Vitamin A 239% • Vitamin C 43%	
Calcium 16% • Iron 30%	

*Percent Daily Values are based on a 2,000 calorie diet.

BREAKFAST BURRITO

SERVES: 1

- 1 corn tortilla or wholemeal if you cannot get corn
- ¼ - ½ block hard tofu, depending on how much filling you like, drained
- 4 mushrooms chopped
- ¼ onion chopped
- 5 cherry tomatoes, halved
- 1 handful spinach
- 100g vegan cheese
- 1 scoop plain protein powder
- 1 tablespoon nutritional yeast
- ¼ teaspoon turmeric
- 1 pinch of ground cumin
- 1 pinch garlic powder
- ½ sliced avocado
- 1 tablespoon parsley

DIRECTIONS

In a non-stick pan, add a splash of water and sauté the onion and mushrooms until just soft. Add the remaining ingredients except the avocado, tortilla and parsley. Mash in the tofu until cooked. Season to taste. Wrap it up in a tortilla with avocado and parsley on top. Serve with salsa, wrap and breakfast is served!

Nutrition Facts

Servings: 1

Amount Per Serving

Calories 632

	% Daily Value*
Total Fat 33.3g	43%
Saturated Fat 8.4g	42%
Trans Fat 0g	
Cholesterol 0mg	0%
Sodium 690mg	30%
Potassium 1442mg	31%
Total Carb 44.9g	15%
Dietary Fiber 15g	54%
Sugars 5.4g	
Protein 45.6g	

Vitamin A 126% • Vitamin C 63%
Calcium 14% • Iron 81%

*Percent Daily Values are based on a 2,000 calorie diet.

BREAKFASTS

COCONUT CREAM PROTEIN SHAKE

SERVES: 1 SHAKE

- 1 frozen banana
- 180 ml unsweetened plant milk (Don't use rice milk which is too thin)
- 1 scoop protein powder
- 1 tablespoon coconut oil
- ½ teaspoon chia seeds
- 2 tablespoons unsweetened coconut flakes + additional for topping
- 170g or ½ cup ice
- 1 tablespoon coconut cream (optional topping)

DIRECTIONS

Place banana, coconut milk, protein powder, coconut oil, coconut flakes, and ice into a high-powered blender and blend until creamy.

For whipped topping, add coconut cream to small bowl and whip with electric mixer until fluffy. Dollop on shake and dust with more coconut flakes.

Nutrition Facts

Servings: 1

Amount Per Serving

Calories 494

	% Daily Value*
Total Fat 28.2g	36%
Saturated Fat 21g	10.5%
Trans Fat 0g	
Cholesterol 65mg	23%
Sodium 83mg	4%
Potassium 679mg	14%
Total Carb 34.7g	12%
Dietary Fiber 6.3g	23%
Sugars 16.5g	
Protein 30.7g	

| Vitamin A 3% | • | Vitamin C 18% |
| Calcium 25% | • | Iron 14% |

*Percent Daily Values are based on a 2,000 calorie diet.

www.thesculptedvegan.com

OVERNIGHT BIRCHER WITH BLUEBERRIES

SERVES: 1

- 50g oats
- 1 tablespoon chia seeds
- ½ tablespoon pumpkin seeds
- 175ml non-dairy milk
- ½ tablespoon maple syrup (omit if cutting calories)
- a squeeze of lemon juice
- a dash of vanilla extract
- 50g blueberries

DIRECTIONS

The night before, put the oats, chia seeds and pumpkin seeds into a bowl, pour over the milk and whisk well. Add the maple syrup, vanilla and lemon juice. Mix well and place in the fridge overnight.

To serve, sprinkle with blueberries, almonds and a sprinkle of cinnamon. (Not included in Nutrition Facts)

Nutrition Facts

Servings: 1

Amount Per Serving	
Calories 382	
	% Daily Value*
Total Fat 10.6g	14%
Saturated Fat 1.4g	7%
Trans Fat 0g	
Cholesterol 0mg	0%
Sodium 101mg	4%
Potassium 300mg	6%
Total Carb 59.8g	20%
Dietary Fiber 10.2g	37%
Sugars 18.2g	
Protein 14.8g	
Vitamin A 31%	Vitamin C 27%
Calcium 24%	Iron 32%

*Percent Daily Values are based on a 2,000 calorie diet.

SUPER PROTEIN SMOOTHIE

SERVES: 1

- ¼ cup oatmeal
- 200g silken tofu
- 1 1/2 cups almond milk
- 1 banana
- 1 tsp chia seeds
- 8-10 pecan or walnuts
- Sprinkle cinnamon
- Handful of spinach (optional)

DIRECTIONS

Place all the ingredients into a blender and process until smooth.

Nutrition Facts

Servings: 1

Amount Per Serving	
Calories 496	
	% Daily Value*
Total Fat 19.1g	25%
Saturated Fat 2.4g	12%
Trans Fat 0g	
Cholesterol 0mg	0%
Sodium 142mg	6%
Potassium 1635mg	35%
Total Carb 65.3g	22%
Dietary Fiber 10.7g	38%
Sugars 25.3g	
Protein 23g	
Vitamin A 270%	Vitamin C 66%
Calcium 23%	Iron 42%

*Percent Daily Values are based on a 2,000 calorie diet.

SUPER SIMPLE PROTEIN OATMEAL

SERVES: 1
- ½ cup oatmeal
- 30g vanilla protein powder
- 300-400ml non-dairy milk
- 4 dates, chopped
- 1 teaspoon linseeds
- Sprinkle of cinnamon

DIRECTIONS
Place the oats, protein powder, dates and milk in a saucepan and bring to the boil. Reduce the heat and simmer, stirring regularly until the oats are cooked and creamy (about 5 minutes for quick cook oats and 12-15 minutes for jumbo oats). Serve sprinkled with linseeds and a drop of milk, and sprinkled with cinnamon. Some chopped banana is also a winner here.

Nutrition Facts
Servings: 1

Amount Per Serving

Calories 664

	% Daily Value*
Total Fat 10.5g	14%
Saturated Fat 1.5g	7%
Trans Fat 0g	
Cholesterol 0mg	0%
Sodium 216mg	9%
Potassium 409mg	9%
Total Carb 71.5g	24%
Dietary Fiber 10.2g	36%
Sugars 35g	
Protein 49.1g	

Vitamin A 71% • Vitamin C 0%
Calcium 43% • Iron 30%

*Percent Daily Values are based on a 2,000 calorie diet.

ULTIMATE SUPER PROTEIN BREAKFAST

SERVES: 1

- 1 large handful of spinach or 1 scoop of greens powder
- 30g of protein powder
- 6 cubes of ice
- 300ml of coconut water or almond milk

DIRECTIONS

Place all the ingredients in a blender and whizz until smooth. Enjoy!

Nutrition Facts

Servings: 1

Amount Per Serving	
Calories 174	
	% Daily Value*
Total Fat 5.3g	14%
Saturated Fat 0.9g	7%
Trans Fat 0g	
Cholesterol 63mg	0%
Sodium 311mg	9%
Potassium 847mg	9%
Total Carb 7.9g	24%
Dietary Fiber 3.1g	36%
Sugars 1.3g	
Protein 32g	

Vitamin A 287%	•	Vitamin C 40%
Calcium 58%	•	Iron 22%

*Percent Daily Values are based on a 2,000 calorie diet.

TOFU SCRAMBLE WITH CHILI, CORIANDER & GARLIC (under 10 minutes to prepare)

SERVES: 4

- 560g firm tofu, drained and squeezed
- 2 tablespoon coconut oil
- 4 tablespoons tamari or low salt soy sauce
- 2 small bunch of coriander (about 30g)
- 2 medium red chili
- 6 spring onions, finely chopped
- 4 cloves garlic, crushed
- sea salt to taste
- 2 lemons
- Selection of green vegetables such as broccoli, mangetout (snow peas) and green beans

DIRECTIONS

Take the tofu out of the packet and use your hands to squeeze out as much water as you can.

Heat the coconut oil in a large, non-stick fry pan and crumble the tofu in. Add the tamari or soy sauce and cook over a high heat for around 5 minutes, stirring regularly. Then turn down the heat to medium.

Very finely chop the stalks of the coriander and add to the pan with the spring onion, garlic and chilli and cook for another 5 minutes or until the soft. Chop the coriander leaves and add to the pan for another 2 minutes then tip the whole lot into a warm bowl.

Add a little water to the pan (around ½ a centimetre in depth) and throw in the green vegetables. Season with salt then cover with tin foil or a lid, and steam on a high heat for around 3 minutes. Remove the lid, add the mange tout and recover. Cook for another 2 minutes, making sure the water doesn't completely evaporate.

To serve, place the vegetables in a warm shallow bowl and drizzle with liquified coconut oil and lemon juice. Tip the tofu in beside it and either eat as it is or serve with brown rice or quinoa.

Nutrition Facts

Servings: 4

Amount Per Serving	
Calories 235	
	% Daily Value*
Total Fat 13.2g	**17%**
Saturated Fat 7.1g	**36%**
Trans Fat 0g	
Cholesterol 0mg	**0%**
Sodium 1040mg	**45%**
Potassium 634mg	**13%**
Total Carb 18.4g	**6%**
Dietary Fiber 6.2g	**22%**
Sugars 6.7g	
Protein 17.7g	
Vitamin A 49% • Vitamin C 171%	
Calcium 28% • Iron 22%	

*Percent Daily Values are based on a 2,000 calorie diet.

BURGERS

CANNELLINI BEAN PATTIES

SERVES: 6

- 3 x 400g tin cannellini or butter beans, drained and rinsed
- 3 cloves garlic peeled
- 3 shallots, chopped
- 15 tablespoons vegan parmesan cheese
- 3 tablespoons chopped basil
- 3 tablespoons plain flour
- Coconut oil for frying

Nutrition Facts

Servings: 6

Amount Per Serving

Calories 376	
	% Daily Value*
Total Fat 6.9g	22%
Saturated Fat 10.7g	53%
Trans Fat 0g	
Cholesterol 26mg	9%
Sodium 688mg	30%
Potassium 1010mg	21%
Total Carb 43g	18%
Dietary Fiber 10.8g	38%
Sugars 4.1g	
Protein 29.3g	

Vitamin A 24%	•	Vitamin C	80%
Calcium 41%	•	Iron	43%

*Percent Daily Values are based on a 2,000 calorie diet.

DIRECTIONS

Whizz the beans in a food processor or blender with the garlic, shallots, cheese, basil and a little water and place in the fridge for 15 to 60 minutes. The longer you leave them, the better they will retain their shape. Shape the mixture into six little patties. The mixture is soft, so flour your hands.

Fry till golden in shallow oil. Drain on kitchen paper. Serve hot with sliced tomato, pickles, avocado and shredded lettuce.

CHICKPEA BURGERS

SERVES: 6

- 400g can of chickpeas
- 200g can of beans (such as pinto, butter or kidney)
- 1 red onion
- 2 large handfuls of green leaves (spinach, kale, rocket, coriander, mint, parsley etc.)
- 75g bread crumbs or panko crumbs
- 75g vegan protein powder
- 2 x Flax eggs
- 1 ½ teaspoon ground cumin
- 1 ½ teaspoon ground coriander (optional)
- 1 ½ teaspoon chilli powder (optional)
- Salt & pepper to taste
- 1 ½ - 2 ½ tablespoons coconut oil

Nutrition Facts

Servings: 6

Amount Per Serving

Calories 278

	% Daily Value*
Total Fat 8.8g	11%
Saturated Fat 5.3g	27%
Trans Fat 0g	
Cholesterol 0mg	0%
Sodium 474mg	21%
Potassium 276mg	6%
Total Carb 34.5g	11%
Dietary Fiber 6.5g	23%
Sugars 2.5g	
Protein 15.3g	

Vitamin A 1% • Vitamin C 7%
Calcium 5% • Iron 17%

*Percent Daily Values are based on a 2,000 calorie diet.

DIRECTIONS

Chop the onion and sauté gently in olive oil for 5 minutes or until translucent.

Transfer to a bowl and add 80% of the crumbs, the protein powder and onion, spices, flax egg and mix. Make six burger patties and dip them in the remaining breadcrumbs. Transfer to the fridge for 60 minutes. This helps the burgers retain their shape when cooking.

In a pan heat the oil and fry for 3 - 4 minutes each side. Once done remove them and set aside. Serve wedged in between two big lettuce leaves, garnished with tomato, avocado and vegan cheese, onions with a salad on the side.

*Flax Egg recipe
2 tablespoons freshly ground flaxseeds (they make better egg, but pre-ground will do if not available)
6 tablespoons water

Mix the flaxseeds and water together in a small bowl and leave to stand for 15 minutes.

www.thesculptedvegan.com

SPICY TOFU & MUSHROOM BURGER

SERVES: 4

- 400g extra firm tofu, cubed, drained and firmly pressed between two kitchen papers
- 1 onion, grated
- 2 medium carrots, grated
- 100 grams mushrooms
- 2 teaspoons grated ginger
- 2 teaspoons crushed garlic
- 1–2 green chillies, deseeded if you like, finely chopped
- 3 tablespoons chopped coriander leaves
- Finely grated zest of 1 lime
- 2 teaspoons garam masala
- Salt to taste
- Freshly ground black pepper
- Coconut oil
- ½ cup panko crumbs (optional, use as much or as little to bind the burger when shaping)

Nutrition Facts

Servings: 4

Amount Per Serving	
Calories 171	
	% Daily Value*
Total Fat 8.2g	11%
Saturated Fat 4.9g	24%
Trans Fat 0g	
Cholesterol 0mg	0%
Sodium 18mg	1%
Potassium 141mg	3%
Total Carb 22.9g	8%
Dietary Fiber 3g	11%
Sugars 10.4g	
Protein 13.1g	

Vitamin A 28%	•	Vitamin C 1%
Calcium 2%	•	Iron 6%

*Percent Daily Values are based on a 2,000 calorie diet.

DIRECTIONS

Burgers: Microwave the tofu for 2-4 minutes. Press water out as much as you can the more the better. Heat onion and carrot in a tablespoon water in skillet, until just tender and carrots are soft.

Blitz the mushrooms in a food processor. Then add all the ingredients, except the oil, and blitz again until well combined but still with texture. Cover and refrigerate for 30 minutes or so. Divide into eight portions and form each into a burger shape*.

With damp hands, divide mixture into 8 portions and shape into mini burgers or 4 large burgers. Fry on both sides over a medium heat in a large pan until burgers are brown, turning once.

Serve wedged between two big lettuce leaves, garnished with tomato, avocado and vegan cheese, onions with a salad on the side.

VEGAN SLOPPY JOES

SERVES: 6

- 680g hard tofu, drain and squeeze the tofu between your hands
- 1 x tin red kidney beans drained and rinsed
- Coconut oil to fry
- ½ chopped onion
- ½ chopped green pepper
- 1 clove garlic
- 1 teaspoon yellow mustard
- 140ml ketchup
- 40ml barbecue sauce
- 15g dark brown soft sugar
- 1 teaspoon finely chopped chilli
- salt and ground black pepper to taste
- Iceberg lettuce, chopped tomato, vegan shredded cheese to serve

Nutrition Facts

Servings: 6

Amount Per Serving	
Calories 398	
	% Daily Value*
Total Fat 10g	13%
Saturated Fat 6.1g	30%
Trans Fat 0g	
Cholesterol 0mg	0%
Sodium 391mg	17%
Potassium 1134mg	24%
Total Carb 55.4g	18%
Dietary Fiber 11.3g	40%
Sugars 12.4g	
Protein 26.7g	
Vitamin A 12%	Vitamin C 32%
Calcium 15%	Iron 46%

*Percent Daily Values are based on a 2,000 calorie diet.

DIRECTIONS

Chop or grate the tofu into mince like pieces. Heat the oil in a frying pan & fry the tofu on a medium heat, add red kidney beans, breaking the beans with a wooden spoon or masher. Add the onion and green pepper. Drain the liquid off.

Very finely chop the garlic and add it to the pan. Add the mustard, ketchup, barbecue sauce, brown sugar and chilli.

Mix thoroughly, reduce heat, simmer for 30 minutes. Season with salt and pepper to taste.

Place 2 large lettuce leaves on a board, one on top of the other. Place approximately 3-4 tablespoons of the mix in the middle of the leaves, add tomato and cheese and roll, folding the edges. Serve with a mixed green salad such as spinach & rocket.

www.thesculptedvegan.com

TOFU BURGERS
(with crushed tomato salsa and creamy basil dressing)

SERVES: 4

FOR THE BURGERS
- 350 g firm silken tofu
- 1 small white onion, diced
- 1 clove garlic, crushed
- 75 g wholemeal breadcrumbs
- 2 heaped teaspoons Marmite/Vegemite
- 1 teaspoon ground cumin

FOR THE SALSA
- 8 ripe tomatoes
- 1 tablespoon red wine vinegar
- 2 sprigs of fresh basil

FOR THE CREAMY BASIL DRESSING
- 4 tablespoons natural vegan yoghurt
- 1 tablespoon white wine vinegar
- 1 teaspoon Dijon mustard
- 4 sprigs of fresh basil
- ¼ of a fresh red chilli

TO SERVE
- 400 g mixed leaves
- 50g vegan cheese
- 50g gherkins
- 4 soft wholemeal buns

DIRECTIONS

Do not be tempted to skip making the dressings for these burgers. They make a good burger, simply stunning! (And they only take 5 mins).

Wrap the tofu in a clean tea towel or muslin cloth, then squeeze and wring it out to remove the excess liquid (about 4 tablespoons should come out – it's messy, but really important to do this for great burger texture later). Place the onion and garlic in small frying pan with a splash of coconut oil and soften for about 5 minutes over a medium low heat. You just want to sweeten them a little.

Place the tofu in a bowl, scraping it off the tea towel. Add in the onion and garlic, then add the breadcrumbs and Marmite. Mix and scrunch together really well with clean hands, then shape into 4 even-sized patties that'll fit nicely in your buns once cooked. (The mixture will firm up if you leave it to sit for five minutes first)

Roughly chop the tomatoes and put into a dry non-stick frying pan on a high heat with a pinch of black pepper, a splash of water and the vinegar. Squash the tomatoes with a fork, cook for 10 to 15 minutes, or until thick and delicious, then tear in the basil leaves and season to perfection (I sometimes add a pinch of dried red chilli flakes too, for a kick). If you want to plump up your buns, pop them into a warm oven for a few minutes.

Next, pick the basil leaves into a blender and blitz with all the other dressing ingredients and a pinch of salt and pepper until super-smooth. Place 2 teaspoons of oil in a large non-stick frying pan on a medium heat. Place the patties in the pan and cook for 3 minutes on each side, or until golden. Slice or grate the cheese, place on the patties, reduce the heat to low, then cover and leave to melt for 3 to 4 minutes. Spread the tomato sauce into the buns, then sandwich the cheesy burgers and sliced gherkins inside. Toss the salad leaves with half the dressing (save the rest for another day), serve alongside the burgers and enjoy – totally awesome.

Nutrition Facts

Servings: 4

Amount Per Serving

Calories 235

	% Daily Value*
Total Fat 13.2g	17%
Saturated Fat 7.1g	36%
Trans Fat 0g	
Cholesterol 0mg	0%
Sodium 1040mg	45%
Potassium 634mg	13%
Total Carb 18.4g	6%
Dietary Fiber 6.2g	22%
Sugars 6.7g	
Protein 17.7g	

Vitamin A 49%	•	Vitamin C 171%
Calcium 28%	•	Iron 22%

*Percent Daily Values are based on a 2,000 calorie diet.

MAINS

CHILLI TOFU STIR-FRY

SERVES: 4

- 400g rice vermicelli noodles
- 2 fresh red chillies, finely sliced with seeds intact
- 2 garlic cloves, crushed
- 4 cm fresh ginger, finely grated
- 160ml salt reduced tamari or soy sauce
- 700g firm tofu, cut into 2 cm cubes
- 6 teaspoons toasted sesame oil
- 1 medium red pepper, seeds removed and finely sliced
- 200g mushrooms, sliced
- 200g baby corn, sliced
- 240g bok choy, roughly chopped
- 2 tablespoons sesame seeds
- fresh coriander leaves, to serve

DIRECTIONS

Place the noodles in a heatproof bowl and cover with boiling water. Leave to stand for 10 minutes, then loosen with a fork. Drain and refresh under cold running water. Drain well and set aside.

Whisk the chilli, garlic, ginger and tamari or soy sauce together in a shallow bowl. Add the tofu and turn gently to coat well. Cover and place in the fridge for 15 minutes (or longer if you can afford the time) to marinate.

Remove the tofu and reserve the marinade. Heat a wok over a high heat. Add half the sesame oil and carefully swirl it around to coat the sides of the wok. Heat until very hot and then add half the tofu and cook for 3 minutes or until golden, stirring gently with a metal slotted spoon. Transfer to a plate lined with kitchen paper and reheat the wok and repeat with the remaining tofu.

Heat the remaining oil in the wok and add the peppers, mushrooms, baby corn and bok choy and stir fry for 3-4 minutes or until tender and crisp.

Add the tofu and reserved marinade and stir-fry for 1 minute. Add the noodles and toss gently until heated through, taking care not to break the tofu.

To serve, place the stir-fry in four serving bowls and sprinkle with sesame seeds and coriander. Squeeze with a wedge of lime.

Place the rest in a bowl to cool and eat for lunch the next day. This is delicious cold!

Nutrition Facts

Servings: 4

Amount Per Serving

Calories 535

	% Daily Value*
Total Fat 17.7g	23%
Saturated Fat 3g	15%
Trans Fat 0g	
Cholesterol 0mg	0%
Sodium 2024mg	88%
Potassium 2123mg	45%
Total Carb 75.3g	25%
Dietary Fiber 8g	29%
Sugars 11g	
Protein 25.3g	

Vitamin A 124%	•	Vitamin C 157%
Calcium 38%	•	Iron 50%

*Percent Daily Values are based on a 2,000 calorie diet.

MAINS

CRUSHED PUY LENTILS WITH TAHINI AND CUMIN

SERVES: 4

- 700-800g cooked lentils (from a tin or packet is fine)
- 60g vegan butter
- 4 tablespoon coconut oil, plus extra for drizzling
- 6 garlic cloves, crushed
- 2 teaspoons ground cumin
- 8 medium tomatoes (660g), blanched, skinned and cut into 1cm dice
- 50g coriander, chopped
- 120g tahini paste
- 4 tablespoons lemon juice
- 1/2 small red onion (50g), thinly sliced
- 1 teaspoon paprika, to garnish (optional)
- Salt and black pepper

DIRECTIONS

Put the butter and oil in a large sauté pan and place on a medium-high heat. Once the butter melts, add the garlic and cumin to cook for about a minute.

Add the tomatoes, 20g of the coriander and the cooked lentils. Continue to cook and stir for a couple of minutes before adding the tahini, lemon juice and 70ml water, along with 1 teaspoon of salt and a good grind of black pepper

Lower to a medium heat and continue to stir and cook gently for about 5 minutes, until hot and thickened. Using a potato masher, roughly mash the lentils a little so that some are broken up and you get a thick porridge consistency.

Spread the lentils on a flat serving plate and sprinkle with the onion, remaining coriander, chopped avocados and a final drizzle of olive oil. Serve warm with the a sprinkle of paprika and a nice green salad. This would even be nice with some warm sourdough bread.

Nutrition Facts

Servings: 4

Amount Per Serving	
Calories 732	
	% Daily Value*
Total Fat 41.1g	23%
Saturated Fat 6.4g	15%
Trans Fat 0g	
Cholesterol 0mg	0%
Sodium -	-
Potassium 1591mg	34%
Total Carb 80.5g	27%
Dietary Fiber 22.7g	81%
Sugars 11.7g	
Protein 33.7g	
Vitamin A 107%	Vitamin C 83%
Calcium 18%	Iron 65%

*Percent Daily Values are based on a 2,000 calorie diet.

www.thesculptedvegan.com

ITALIAN NO-MEATBALLS

SERVES: 36 BALLS
(freeze remaining portions)

- 1 onion, diced
- Coconut oil, for sautéing (optional)
- 225g mushrooms, quartered
- 2 tablespoons tamari or soy sauce
- 1 tablespoon chickpea miso or white miso
- 490g cooked brown rice
- 90g cooked lentils
- 55g tomato paste
- 3 tablespoons nutritional yeast
- 4 to 6 cloves garlic, minced
- 1½ teaspoon dried basil
- 1 teaspoon fresh rosemary, chopped, or ½ teaspoon dried rosemary
- 45g rolled oats
- 125g ground walnuts (grind in a food processor)

DIRECTIONS

Preheat the oven to 175°C/Gas mark 4.

Line two baking sheets with parchment paper. Heat a deep skillet over medium heat and cook the onions dry (you can sauté in oil as well, if you like), until they begin to stick a bit. Splash them with a bit of water to loosen them from the pan and continue cooking, (adding a bit of water now and then to prevent sticking) until they are tender.

Put the mushrooms into a food processor and pulse until they are finely minced but not reduced to a pulp. Add them to the onion and cook for several minutes, until browned. Stir in the tamari and miso.

Add the brown rice and lentils and mix well. Mix in the tomato paste, nutritional yeast, 4 cloves garlic (or more depending on how garlicky you like it) and herbs. In a blender, process the oats briefly, but not to a flour, and add to the mixture.

Mix the walnuts into the mixture well and form into meatballs. This can be done efficiently using a small ice cream scoop, or your hands.

Place on the baking sheets with 1¼cm of space between them, and bake for 30 to 35 minutes, until browned and they hold their shape. Italian meatballs will keep for 1 week in the refrigerator.

Serve with salad and cooked quinoa, or cook in Bolognese sauce and serve with spaghetti.

Nutrition Facts

Servings: 6

Amount Per Serving

Calories 560

	% Daily Value*
Total Fat 15.8g	20%
Saturated Fat 1.3g	7%
Trans Fat 0g	
Cholesterol 0mg	0%
Sodium 428mg	19%
Potassium 889mg	19%
Total Carb 87.6g	29%
Dietary Fiber 12.3g	44%
Sugars 3.4g	
Protein 21g	

Vitamin A 6%	•	Vitamin C 11%
Calcium 6%	•	Iron 35%

*Percent Daily Values are based on a 2,000 calorie diet.

SMOKY BUTTERNUT SQUASH AND BEAN CASSEROLE, WITH TOMATO SALSA

SERVES: 4

- ½ a butternut squash, approx. 600g
- Coconut oil
- 1 heaped teaspoon ground coriander
- Sea salt & black pepper
- 3 mixed-colour peppers
- 1 heaped teaspoon smoked paprika
- 2 red onions
- 4 cloves of garlic
- 4 fresh bay leaves
- 2 x 400 g tins of black beans, not drained
- 150 g brown rice

FOR THE SALSA

- 2 ripe mixed-colour tomatoes
- ½-1 fresh red chilli
- 1 bunch of fresh coriander, approx. 30g
- 1 lime

DIRECTIONS

Preheat the oven to 200°C/400°F/gas 6.

Halve and deseed the squash, then carefully chop into 3cm chunks. In a large roasting tray, toss and massage it with 1 teaspoon of oil, the ground coriander and a pinch of sea salt and black pepper. Deseed the peppers and cut into 3cm chunks, then, in a separate tray toss and massage them with 1 teaspoon of oil and the smoked paprika. Place both trays in the oven for 35 minutes, or until softened.

Meanwhile, peel and finely chop ¼ of an onion and put aside, then roughly chop the rest and place in a large casserole pan on a low heat with 1 tablespoon of oil. Crush in the garlic, add the bay leaves and a good splash of water and cook for 20 minutes, or until soft, stirring regularly.

Tip in the beans, juice and all, then half-fill each empty tin with water, swirl and pour into the pan. Simmer until the time is up on the squash and peppers, then stir both into the pan. Simmer for a further 20 minutes, or until the casserole is dark and delicious, loosening with an extra splash of water, if needed. Meanwhile, cook the rice according to the packet instructions, then drain.

To make a quick salsa, deseed the tomatoes, then finely chop with as much chilli as you like and most of the coriander leaves. Scrape into a bowl with the reserved finely chopped onion and toss with the lime juice, then season to perfection.

Serve the casserole with the rice and salsa, a spoonful of vegan crème fraiche and a sprinkling of the remaining coriander leaves.

Nutrition Facts

Servings: 4

Amount Per Serving	
Calories 400	
	% Daily Value*
Total Fat 75.7g	7%
Saturated Fat 0.8g	4%
Trans Fat 0g	
Cholesterol 0mg	0%
Sodium 462mg	20%
Potassium 1396mg	30%
Total Carb 79.8g	27%
Dietary Fiber 13.1g	47%
Sugars 9.3g	
Protein 12.9g	

Vitamin A 580%	•	Vitamin C 90%
Calcium 15%	•	Iron 29%

*Percent Daily Values are based on a 2,000 calorie diet.

SPICED CAULIFLOWER & CHICKPEA CURRY

SERVES: 4

- 6 teaspoons coconut oil
- 1 small brown onion, finely chopped
- 4 garlic cloves, crushed
- 4cm fresh ginger, peeled and grated
- 1 teaspoon ground coriander
- 2 teaspoons ground cumin
- 2 teaspoons garam masala
- 4 teaspoons ground turmeric
- pinch of dried chilli flakes
- 300g tinned chopped tomatoes
- 400ml salt-reduced vegetable stock
- 300g cauliflower, cut into florets
- 3 x 400g cans chickpeas drained and rinsed
- 1 cup light coconut milk
- 60g frozen peas
- salt and pepper to taste
- 4 tablespoons chopped coriander

DIRECTIONS

Heat the oil in a large skillet or saucepan over a medium heat. Add the onion, garlic and ginger and cook for 5 minutes or until the onion is soft and translucent. Add the ground coriander, cumin, garam masala, turmeric and chilli flakes. Cook for a further 2-3 minutes or until fragrant, stirring constantly.

Stir in the tomatoes, stock, cauliflower, chickpeas, coconut milk and peas and bring to the boil over a high heat. Reduce the heat to medium-low and simmer, covered for around 15 minutes.

Remove the lid and cook for a further 5 minutes or until the sauce has thickened a little, stirring occasionally. Season with salt and pepper.

To serve, sprinkle over the coriander and serve with a lime wedge, some mango chutney and perhaps a dollop of vegan sour cream. Delicious! Save the rest for lunch the next day.

Nutrition Facts

Servings: 4

Amount Per Serving

Calories 657

	% Daily Value*
Total Fat 27g	7%
Saturated Fat 18.5g	4%
Trans Fat 0g	
Cholesterol 0mg	0%
Sodium 753mg	20%
Potassium 1399mg	30%
Total Carb 89g	27%
Dietary Fiber 22.7g	47%
Sugars 26.2g	
Protein 20.9g	

| Vitamin A 189% | • | Vitamin C 109% |
| Calcium 14% | • | Iron 47% |

*Percent Daily Values are based on a 2,000 calorie diet.

THAI PEANUT TOFU WITH MIX VEG BOWL

SERVES: 4

THAI PEANUT SAUCE
- 175g unsalted, unsweetened peanut butter
- 4 tablespoons low-sodium tamari or liquid aminos
- 4 tablespoons maple syrup
- 2 tablespoons sriracha
- 1 tablespoon lime juice
- 1 tablespoon toasted sesame oil, optional
- 1 teaspoon fresh grated ginger
- 1 packs of 400g block extra-firm tofu, cubed
- 1/2 head of broccoli, broken into florets and stems sliced
- 1 sweet potatoes cubed
- 2 tablespoons low-sodium tamari or liquid aminos
- 1 tablespoon maple syrup
- 1 tablespoon sesame oil
- 2 tablespoon coconut oil
- Black pepper to taste
- 225g very thinly sliced red cabbage
- 75g chopped peanuts
- 2 onions, chopped
- 2 tablespoons (30g) chopped coriander

DIRECTIONS

Drain and squeeze the tofu between your hands wrapped in kitchen paper.

Preheat the oven to 200C/400F/Gas mark 6. Line a baking sheet with parchment paper and set aside.

In a small bowl, combine the ingredients for the Thai Peanut Sauce and whisk until thoroughly combined and smooth. Place the tofu cubes in a medium shallow bowl and top with 1/3 of the peanut sauce. Stir until combined. Let the tofu marinate for about 15 minutes.

While the tofu is marinating, prepare the broccoli by tipping the broccoli florets and stems into a big bowl with the sweet potato. In a small cup, stir together the tamari/liquid aminos, maple syrup, and sesame oil. Pour it over the vegetables and toss until coated. Roast, spread out on the baking sheet in the oven for 20 minutes, tossing once after 10 minutes.

While the veggies are roasting, cook your tofu. Heat the coconut oil in a frying pan, over medium heat. Add the tofu, 1/3 of the sauce, to the pan and cook, stirring occasionally (gently scraping the pan as necessary), until the sauce has cooked away and the tofu is browned and slightly crispy. Remove from the heat. Add pepper to taste.

To assemble the bowls, divide the sweet potatoes, broccoli, red cabbage, and tofu amongst the bowls. Drizzle generously with the remainder of the peanut sauce. Sprinkle with scallions spring onions, coriander, and chopped peanuts. Serve immediately.

Nutrition Facts

Servings: 8

Amount Per Serving	
Calories 540	
	% Daily Value*
Total Fat 36.9g	**47%**
Saturated Fat 8.6g	**43%**
Trans Fat 0g	
Cholesterol 0mg	**0%**
Sodium 1549mg	**67%**
Potassium 694mg	**15%**
Total Carb 40g	**13%**
Dietary Fiber 8.1g	**29%**
Sugars 22.7g	
Protein 22.9g	
Vitamin A 244% • Vitamin C 157%	
Calcium 23% • Iron 24%	

*Percent Daily Values are based on a 2,000 calorie diet.

THE BEST VEGAN MEDITERRANEAN QUICHE IN THE WORLD

SERVES: 4

FOR THE CRUST
- 90g quick cook oats
- 140g sunflower seeds
- 1 teaspoon dried oregano
- 1 tablespoon coconut oil
- ¼ teaspoon salt

FOR THE FILLING
- Coconut oil
- 2 large cloves garlic, finely chopped
- 1 red onion, finely diced
- 3 spring onions, finely sliced
- 10 black olives, finely sliced
- 5 sun-dried tomatoes in oil, finely chopped
- a handful of fresh basil, finely chopped
- 1 teaspoon fresh rosemary, finely chopped
- 2 tablespoons nutritional yeast flakes
- 400g firm silken tofu

DIRECTIONS

Preheat the oven to 175C/350F/gas mark 4

To make the crust, blitz the oats and sunflower seeds in a food processor to a flour-like consistency. Mix in the oregano, oil and salt. Use your hands to knead the mixture into a dough. Add water as necessary to make the dough soft and pliable.

Lightly oil a 20cm quiche tin and spread out the dough to cover the bottom of the tin, using your fingers to press it down firmly and evenly to the edges. Then use a fork to pierce the dough all over. Bake for approximately 15 minutes or until firm to the touch.

In the meantime, make the filling. Heat a drizzle of oil in a frying pan and sauté the garlic, onion and spring onions for several minutes until soft. Turn off the heat and add all the other ingredients, apart from the tofu.

Take the tofu between both hands and squeeze it over the sink to get as much liquid as you can out of it. Place the squeezed tofu into a food processor, add 1 tablespoon of oil and blitz until the tofu has a smooth, creamy consistency. Transfer to the pan with the other ingredients and stir until well combined.

Spoon the mixture onto the cooked quiche crust and bake in the oven for about 30 minutes or until firm to touch and slightly browned on top.

Serve with a big green salad on the side.

Nutrition Facts

Servings: 4

Amount Per Serving	
Calories 553	
	% Daily Value*
Total Fat 36.3g	46%
Saturated Fat 3.8g	19%
Trans Fat 0g	
Cholesterol 0mg	0%
Sodium 591mg	26%
Potassium 1034mg	22%
Total Carb 56g	19%
Dietary Fiber 15.4g	55%
Sugars 17.3g	
Protein 27.7g	
Vitamin A 51% • Vitamin C 51%	
Calcium 23% • Iron 38%	

*Percent Daily Values are based on a 2,000 calorie diet.

VEGAN MEXICAN CHILLI

SERVES: 6

- 2 medium-sized sweet potatoes, approximately 500g
- 1 level tsp cayenne pepper, plus extra for sprinkling
- 1 heaped tsp ground cumin, plus extra for sprinkling
- 1 level tsp ground cinnamon, plus extra for sprinkling
- 1 heaped tsp smoked paprika, plus extra for sprinkling
- sea salt
- freshly ground black pepper
- coconut oil
- 1 onion
- 1 red pepper
- 1 yellow pepper
- 2 cloves garlic
- a bunch of fresh coriander
- 1 fresh red chilli
- 1 fresh green chilli
- 2 x 400 g tinned beans, such as kidney, chickpea, pinto and cannellini
- 2 x 400 g tinned chopped tomatoes

DIRECTIONS

Preheat the oven to 200°C/400°F/gas 6. Peel the sweet potatoes and cut into bite-sized chunks. Sprinkle with a pinch each of cayenne, cumin, cinnamon, paprika, salt and pepper. Drizzle with coconut oil and toss to coat, then spread out on a baking tray and place in the hot oven for 30 minutes, or until soft and golden.

Peel and roughly chop the onion. Halve, deseed and roughly chop the peppers. Peel and finely chop the garlic. Pick the coriander leaves and put aside, then finely chop the stalks. Deseed and finely chop the chillies.

Meanwhile, put a large pan over a medium-high heat and add the coconut oil. Add the onion, peppers and garlic and cook for 5 minutes. Add the coriander stalks, chilli and spices and cook for another 5 to 10 minutes, or until softened, stirring every couple of minutes.

Drain the beans, then tip them into the pan with the tinned tomatoes. Stir well and bring to the boil, then reduce to a medium-low heat and leave to tick away for 25 to 30 minutes, or until thickened and reduced. Keep an eye on it, and add a splash of water if it gets a bit thick.

Stir the roasted sweet potato through your chilli with most of the coriander leaves. Taste and season with salt and pepper, if you think it needs it.

Scatter the remaining leaves over the top, and serve with some vegan soured cream, vegan cheese, guacamole or chopped avocado and coriander leaves. This dish is especially good when made a day in advance.

Nutrition Facts

Servings: 6

Amount Per Serving	
Calories 546	
	% Daily Value*
Total Fat 6.5g	8%
Saturated Fat 2.7g	13%
Trans Fat 0g	
Cholesterol 0mg	0%
Sodium 415mg	18%
Potassium 1673mg	36%
Total Carb 97.5g	32%
Dietary Fiber 33.6g	120%
Sugars 17.9g	
Protein 25.8g	
Vitamin A 200% • Vitamin C 99%	
Calcium 6% • Iron 13%	

*Percent Daily Values are based on a 2,000 calorie diet.

VEGAN MOUSSAKA

SERVES: 4

- 2 large aubergines, thinly sliced
- 1 medium onion, finely diced
- 2 garlic cloves, crushed
- 2 carrots, coarsely grated
- 2 teaspoons dried oregano
- ½ teaspoon ground cinnamon
- 400g tinned chopped tomatoes
- 1 cup reduced salt vegetable stock
- 900g tinned brown lentils, drained and rinsed
- 2 large white potatoes, peeled
- 80g vegan cheddar cheese
- Salt and pepper to taste

DIRECTIONS

Preheat the oven to 180°C/350°F/gas 5.

Place the sliced aubergine in a colander and sprinkle liberally with salt, coating each slice. Cover with a couple of layers of kitchen paper and place a wide bowl on top, followed by several heavy dinner plates. Leave like this for one hour, if you have time. The goal here is for the salt to draw the moisture and bitterness out of the aubergines, and the weights to help to squeeze them.

After an hour, squeeze each slice gently with some kitchen paper and place on baking trays lined with baking paper. Bake in the oven (in batches if necessary) for 15-20 minutes until tender. Set aside to cool slightly.

Meanwhile, heat some coconut oil in a large skillet or pan and cook the onion, garlic and carrot for 5 minutes until soft and translucent. Add the oregano and cook for a further minute.

Stir in the tomatoes, stock, cinnamon and lentils and season well with salt and pepper. Reduce the heat to medium-low and simmer, covered for 15 minutes, stirring occasionally.

Place the potatoes (whole) into a saucepan with enough boiling water to cover, and add a teaspoon of salt. Bring to the boil, turn down the heat and simmer for 15 minutes or until tender. When cool enough to handle, cut into 5 mm thick slices.

Spread a large spoonful of the lentil mixture over the base of a large baking dish. Layer half of the aubergine over the top, followed by another layer of the lentil mixture. Repeat the layers again, finishing with the lentil mixture on top.

Arrange the potato slices over top, season well and sprinkle with grated vegan cheese.

Bake in the oven for 30 minutes or until the potato is golden and serve with a crisp green salad.

Nutrition Facts

Servings: 4

Amount Per Serving	
Calories 546	
	% Daily Value*
Total Fat 6.5g	8%
Saturated Fat 2.7g	13%
Trans Fat 0g	
Cholesterol 0mg	0%
Sodium 415mg	18%
Potassium 1673mg	36%
Total Carb 97.5g	32%
Dietary Fiber 33.6g	120%
Sugars 17.9g	
Protein 25.8g	

Vitamin A 200%	•	Vitamin C 99%	
Calcium 6%	•	Iron 13%	

*Percent Daily Values are based on a 2,000 calorie diet.

SALADS

BEANSPROUT & MANGO SALAD WITH AGAVE CASHEWS

SERVES: 4-6

- 2 bunches of fresh coriander (approx 180g)
- 2 x 400g bag of beansprouts
- 200g cashew nuts
- 2 teaspoons agave syrup
- 2 tablespoons coconut oil
- 1 fresh red chilli

DRESSING

- 2 small ripe mangos
- 2 teaspoons soy sauce
- 2 teaspoons sesame oil
- 2 limes or 1 lemon

Nutrition Facts

Servings: 4

Amount Per Serving	
Calories 610	
	% Daily Value*
Total Fat 42.6g	55%
Saturated Fat 12.5g	62%
Trans Fat 0g	
Cholesterol 0mg	0%
Sodium 196mg	9%
Potassium 1005mg	21%
Total Carb 51.9g	17%
Dietary Fiber 8.8g	31%
Sugars 27.9g	
Protein 14g	

Vitamin A 197% • Vitamin C 100%
Calcium 7% • Iron 26%

*Percent Daily Values are based on a 2,000 calorie diet.

DIRECTIONS

To make the salad, pick the leaves of the coriander and put them in a large bowl. Finely slice the stalks then add to the bowl with the beansprouts and set aside. Put a large frying pan on a low heat and wrap the cashews in a tea towel. Give them a whack with a rolling pin to bash them up, then put into the frying pan. Add coconut oil and leave to toast, tossing occasionally until golden. Remove the pan from the heat and add a good drizzle of agave syrup, toss and set aside.

Finely slice the chilli, peel the mango and chip away at the flesh to form chunks and pieces. Add to the salad with the chilli. Make a dressing with glugs of soy sauce, coconut and sesame oil, and the juice of 1 lime or lemon. Toss and then add the cashew nuts at the end. Tuck in and enjoy!

CARROT AND MUNG BEAN SALAD

SERVES: 4

- 140g dried green mung beans
- 60ml olive oil, plus extra for drizzling
- 1 teaspoon cumin seeds
- 1 teaspoon caraway seeds
- 1 teaspoon fennel seeds
- 2 garlic cloves, crushed
- 2 tablespoons white wine vinegar
- large pinch of chilli flakes
- 1 teaspoon salt
- 3 large carrots, peeled and cut into 5cm x 1cm batons
- 150 ml of water
- ½ teaspoon caster sugar
- 20g coriander, chopped
- grated zest of 1 lemon
- 140g vegan feta, broken into chunks (omit if you like)

Nutrition Facts

Servings: 4

Amount Per Serving

Calories 255

	% Daily Value*
Total Fat 18.4g	24%
Saturated Fat 4.5g	23%
Trans Fat 0g	
Cholesterol 13mg	5%
Sodium 467mg	20%
Potassium 235mg	5%
Total Carb 14.4g	5%
Dietary Fiber 3.4g	12%
Sugars 3.3g	
Protein 19.7g	

Vitamin A 329%	•	Vitamin C 9%
Calcium 9%	•	Iron 5%

*Percent Daily Values are based on a 2,000 calorie diet.

DIRECTIONS

Bring a medium saucepan of water to the boil, add the mung beans and simmer for 20-25 minutes, until the beans are cooked but still retain a bite. Drain, shake well and transfer to a large mixing bowl. About 3 minutes before the beans are cooked, heat 2 tablespoons of olive oil in a small frying pan and add the cumin, caraway and fennel seeds.

Cook on a medium heat, stirring often, until the seeds start to pop – about 3 minutes. Pour the oil and seeds over the hot beans, and add the garlic, vinegar, chilli flakes and ½ teaspoon of the salt. Set aside to cool.

While the beans are cooking, place the carrots in a pan large enough to form a shallow layer and pour over the water, along with the remaining oil, sugar and ½ teaspoon salt. Bring to a rapid boil and cook for 10-12 minutes, by which time all the water should have evaporated and the carrots are slightly caramelised whilst remaining slightly al dente.

Drain some liquid if needed. Add the carrots to the mung beans along with the coriander, and stir gently. Transfer to plates, sprinkle over the lemon zest, dot with vegan feta (if using) and finish with a drizzle of olive oil.

SPINACH, PEACH AND PECAN SALAD

SERVES: 6

- 55g pecans
- 55g walnuts
- 110g cooked edamame beans
- 3 ripe peaches or 1 tin of peaches, drained & cut into bite sized pieces
- 1 ½ bags ready-washed spinach
- 6 tablespoons vinaigrette

Nutrition Facts

Servings: 6

Amount Per Serving

Calories 261

	% Daily Value*
Total Fat 22g	28%
Saturated Fat 2.6g	13%
Trans Fat 0g	
Cholesterol 0mg	0%
Sodium 0mg	0%
Potassium 230mg	5%
Total Carb 10.8g	4%
Dietary Fiber 5.2g	18%
Sugars 8.4g	
Protein 8.3g	

| Vitamin A 180% | • | Vitamin C 10% |
| Calcium 2% | • | Iron 6% |

*Percent Daily Values are based on a 2,000 calorie diet.

DIRECTIONS

Preheat oven to 180ºC/360ºF/gas 5. Arrange pecans & walnuts in a single layer on a baking tray and roast in preheated oven for 5 to 10 minutes, until they just begin to darken. Remove from oven and set aside.

If using fresh peaches, peel peaches (if desired), remove stones and slice into bite-sized pieces. Combine peaches, spinach, edamame beans and cooled nuts in a large bowl. Divide into bowls, toss with a dressing of your choice until evenly coated. Serve immediately

CITRUS TOFU SALAD WITH AVOCADO

SERVES: 4

TOFU MARINADE AND DRESSING
- 2 medium oranges
- 2 lemons
- 2 limes
- 1 teaspoon minced garlic
- 1 small diced onion
- 1 - 2 teaspoons cumin
- 120ml coconut oil
- Coconut oil to fry
- 2 tablespoons agave or maple syrup
- 2 tablespoons fresh herbs (coriander or parsley)
- Salt and pepper to taste

SALAD
- 2 packs (approx 280g per pack) cubed hard tofu, drain and squeeze the tofu between your hands
- 2 bags of mixed lettuce leaves
- 2 large avocados sliced
- 4 or more Tangerines/ Mandarins / Clementine, peeled (adjust quantity to taste)
- 2 red peppers sliced

Nutrition Facts

Servings: 4

Amount Per Serving

Calories 405

	% Daily Value*
Total Fat 28.9g	37%
Saturated Fat 14.6g	73%
Trans Fat 0g	
Cholesterol 0mg	0%
Sodium 58mg	3%
Potassium 479mg	10%
Total Carb 28.8g	10%
Dietary Fiber 8.6g	31%
Sugars 10.3g	
Protein 12.9g	

Vitamin A 10%	•	Vitamin C 117%
Calcium 10%	•	Iron 16%

*Percent Daily Values are based on a 2,000 calorie diet.

DIRECTIONS

Squeeze out juice from orange, lemon and lime into a non-reactive pan. Add cumin, agave or maple syrup, garlic, onion, oil and herbs. Whisk everything together then lightly salt and pepper to taste. Mix well to combine, adjust for seasoning. Marinade tofu with about half of the marinade make sure to coat all sides.

Marinade for about for about 30 minutes. Heat a frying pan. Coat with coconut oil add the peppers and cook for about 3 minutes. Remove from the pan, and set aside. Lightly wipe pan.

Coat pan with oil. Add the tofu to pan; fry until done.

In a large plate or bowl, arrange the lettuce, tofu, sliced avocados, oranges and pepper. Serve with citrus dressing on the side.

www.thesculptedvegan.com

MANGO AND CURRIED CHICKPEA SALAD

SERVES: 4

- 400g tinned chickpeas, drained and rinsed
- 1 teaspoon coriander seeds
- 1 teaspoon black mustard seeds
- ½ teaspoon cumin seeds
- 1 teaspoon curry powder
- ½ teaspoon ground turmeric
- 1 teaspoon caster sugar
- 80ml coconut oil
- 1 large onion, thinly sliced
- 1 small cauliflower, broken into 4cm florets
- 1 large ripe mango, peeled and cut into 2cm dice
- 1 medium-hot green chilli, deseeded and finely chopped
- 20g coriander, chopped
- 3 tablespoons lime juice
- 50g baby spinach leaves
- salt

Nutrition Facts

Servings: 4

Amount Per Serving	
Calories 478	
	% Daily Value*
Total Fat 23g	29%
Saturated Fat 16.4g	82%
Trans Fat 0g	
Cholesterol 0mg	0%
Sodium 87mg	4%
Potassium 1053mg	22%
Total Carb 59.3g	20%
Dietary Fiber 15g	54%
Sugars 22.8g	
Protein 22.7g	
Vitamin A 58% • Vitamin C 117%	
Calcium 9% • Iron 29%	

*Percent Daily Values are based on a 2,000 calorie diet.

DIRECTIONS

Place the coriander, mustard and cumin seeds in a large frying pan and dry-roast them over a medium heat until they begin to pop. Use a spice grinder or pestle and mortar to crush them to a powder and then add them to the curry powder, turmeric, sugar and ½ teaspoon of salt. Set aside. (You can also use the milling blade and small cup of a Nutribullet or similar blender)

In the same pan, add half the oil and cook the onion for 5 minutes on a high heat, stirring occasionally, so that it starts to gain some colour. Add the spice mix and keep cooking on a medium heat for another 5 minutes, until the onion is completely soft. Transfer to the bowl with the chickpeas and keep aside.

Bring a large pot of water to the boil, throw in the cauliflower and blanch for just 1 minute. Drain, pan dry and set aside. Once the cauliflower is completely dry, heat up the remaining oil in the same pan you cooked the onion in (you don't need to clean it), add the cauliflower, along with ¼ teaspoon of salt, and fry on a high heat for 3-4 minutes, just to give it colour.

Add the hot cauliflower and any oil from the pan to the onion and chickpeas and stir well. Leave to stand for 5 minutes if you want the salad warm, or longer if you want it at room temperature. Add the mango to the salad, along with the chilli, coriander, lime juice and spinach. Stir well and serve at once or chill and serve within 24 hours.

MUSHROOM MELT WITH GREEN SALAD

SERVES: 4

- 1 small brown onion, thinly sliced
- 2 garlic cloves, crushed
- 1 tablespoon chopped fresh thyme
- 400g white mushrooms, sliced
- 1 tablespoon chopped fresh parsley
- salt and pepper to taste
- 80g of vegan mozzarella, grated (if you can can't find it, any vegan cheese will do)
- 400g tinned cannellini beans, drained and rinsed
- 1 teaspoon ground cumin
- 2 tablespoons lemon juice
- 4 slices of sourdough bread
- handfuls of rocket leaves

Nutrition Facts

Servings: 4

Amount Per Serving	
Calories 535	
	% Daily Value*
Total Fat 6.3g	8%
Saturated Fat 0.4g	2%
Trans Fat 0g	
Cholesterol 0mg	0%
Sodium 429mg	19%
Potassium 1827mg	39%
Total Carb 90g	30%
Dietary Fiber 28.1g	100%
Sugars 6.1g	
Protein 32.7g	
Vitamin A 4%	Vitamin C 24%
Calcium 28%	Iron 75%

*Percent Daily Values are based on a 2,000 calorie diet.

DIRECTIONS

Heat a non-stick frying pan over a medium heat and drizzle with cooking coconut oil. Add the onion and cook for 5 minutes until soft and translucent. Add the garlic and thyme and cook for 1 minute or until fragrant, stirring constantly. Add the mushrooms and cook for 10 minutes until soft. Remove from the heat and drain off any excess liquid.

Stir in the parsley and season with salt and pepper. Set aside to cool completely. Once cooled, add the vegan cheese and gently stir to combine.

Place the cannellini beans, cumin and lemon juice in a small bowl and roughly mash with a fork until a chunky paste has formed. Add a little cold water if it seems too thick.

Place a slice of bread on a chopping board and spread over the bean mixture. Layer the mushroom mixture and rocket. Top with another slice of bread.

Place the sandwich either in a sandwich press or in a clean, hot frying pan. Toast for 3-5 minutes (flipping half way through if in a pan) or until the sandwich is golden.

To serve, place on a serving plate with a large green salad on the side.

Keep half of the mixture to make another toastie for lunch the next day. Or simply serve with steamed green vegetables, or topped onto an oven baked sweet potato.

www.thesculptedvegan.com

SALADS

CAULIFLOWER BITES & MEXICAN STREET SALAD

SERVES: 2-4
- 1 large head of cauliflower
- 2 tablespoons coconut oil
- ½ teaspoon of salt
- 2 tablespoon nutritional yeast
- 1 teaspoon garlic powder (not garlic salt)
- 1 teaspoon chili powder

MEXICAN STREET SALAD
SERVES: 4
- ½ small white cabbage
- ½ small red cabbage
- 1 small bunch radishes, (about 10) trimmed and finely sliced
- 2 carrots, peeled and finely sliced
- 1 large bunch fresh coriander, leaves and stalks finely chopped
- 2 large jalapeno chillies (or other green chilli), to taste, finely sliced
- 1 red onion, peeled and finely sliced
- extra virgin olive oil
- juice of 2-3 limes
- sea salt

DIRECTIONS
Preheat oven to 230°C/450°F/gas mark 8. Chop the cauliflower into little florets and add to a big bowl. Add all of the seasonings, the oil, salt to taste, nutritional yeast, garlic powder and chili powder. Toss well to combine and to evenly coat the cauliflower. Spread the cauliflower evenly on a baking sheet and bake 20 minutes, flipping once half way through. The cauliflower is done when it is browned and tender. Serve with a Mexican street salad, either hot or cold.

Mexican Street Salad
This simple little salad can be quite extraordinary, but you've got to season it with that Mexican spirit by being brave with the lime juice, salt and chilli, until it's singing in your mouth. It does a great job of waking up the other things it's served.

The easiest and quickest way to make this is to use a food processor with a slicer attachment or a mandolin. If you don't have either of those, use a speed peeler, or simply grate everything finely.

Shred your white and red cabbage into two separate piles. Put just the white cabbage into a large bowl with the radishes, carrots and most of the coriander. Mix everything together well, then kick up the flavours by adding almost all the chopped chilli, the sliced red onion and a good few lugs of liquified coconut oil. Add most of the lime juice and a good pinch of salt, then toss together and have a taste. Just keep adjusting everything, adding more fragrance with the coriander, heat with the last of the chilli and acid with another squeeze of lime juice, until it's just right for you.

When you're happy, fold in the red cabbage right before serving so it doesn't stain everything, and tuck in. Serve with scrambled tofu for an extra protein hit.

Nutrition Facts

Servings: 4

Amount Per Serving	
Calories 196	
	% Daily Value*
Total Fat 11.2g	14%
Saturated Fat 1.6g	8%
Trans Fat 0g	
Cholesterol 0mg	0%
Sodium 361mg	16%
Potassium 783mg	17%
Total Carb 24.7g	8%
Dietary Fiber 9.7g	35%
Sugars 10.1g	
Protein 6g	
Vitamin A 42% • Vitamin C 203%	
Calcium 20% • Iron 13%	

*Percent Daily Values are based on a 2,000 calorie diet.

www.thesculptedvegan.com

SLOW COOKER

SLOW COOKER BALSAMIC TOFU

SERVES: 4

- 450g Brussels sprouts, trimmed and halved
- 450g red potatoes, halved or quartered if large
- 400g hard tofu, drained and pressed between your hands
- 120 ml balsamic vinegar
- 60 ml vegetable stock
- 75g brown sugar
- 2 tablespoons grainy Dijon mustard
- 2 teaspoons dried thyme
- 2 teaspoons dried rosemary
- 1 teaspoon dried oregano
- 1 teaspoon crushed red pepper flakes
- Salt
- Freshly ground black pepper
- 2 cloves garlic, minced
- Freshly chopped parsley, for garnish

Nutrition Facts

Servings: 4

Amount Per Serving	
Calories 244	
	% Daily Value*
Total Fat 1.2g	1%
Saturated Fat 0.3g	1%
Trans Fat 0g	
Cholesterol 0mg	0%
Sodium 167mg	7%
Potassium 1037mg	22%
Total Carb 54.3g	18%
Dietary Fiber 7.3g	26%
Sugars 22g	
Protein 17.1g	

Vitamin A 47%	•	Vitamin C 186%
Calcium 8%	•	Iron 21%

*Percent Daily Values are based on a 2,000 calorie diet.

DIRECTIONS

In a large slow cooker, add Brussels sprouts and potatoes in an even layer and place tofu on top.

In a small bowl, whisk together balsamic vinegar, vegetable stock, brown sugar, mustard, dried thyme, rosemary, and oregano, and crushed red pepper flakes. Season generously with salt and pepper.

Pour marinade over tofu and vegetables. Scatter all over with garlic. Cover and cook on high 4 ½ to 5 hours. Garnish with parsley and serve with the juices.

SLOW COOKER BEAN & SPINACH GOULASH

SERVES: 4

- 1 x 400g can red kidney beans, drained and rinsed
- 1 x 400g can butter beans, drained and rinsed
- 1 x 400g can chickpeas, drained and rinsed
- 1 x 400 g can black eye beans, drained and rinsed
- 3 onions, diced
- 800g tin chopped tomatoes
- 2 red peppers, diced
- 1 heaped teaspoon smoked paprika
- 1 whole bulb of garlic cloves, peeled but left whole
- 1 teaspoon of Vegemite or Marmite
- 3 heaped teaspoons cornflour mixed with a little cold water
- 300g bag of spinach
- 1 sweet potato to serve

Nutrition Facts

Servings: 4

Amount Per Serving

Calories 476

	% Daily Value*
Total Fat 2.6g	3%
Saturated Fat 0.2g	1%
Trans Fat 0g	
Cholesterol 0mg	0%
Sodium 893mg	39%
Potassium 997mg	21%
Total Carb 101.9g	34%
Dietary Fiber 38.3g	137%
Sugars 17.4g	
Protein 34.9g	

Vitamin A 246% • Vitamin C 119%
Calcium 13% • Iron 29%

*Percent Daily Values are based on a 2,000 calorie diet.

DIRECTIONS

Pile all the ingredients except the cornflour and spinach in the slow cooker.

Stir and cook for 4 hours on high or 6 – 8 hours on low. Pour in the cornflour mix and stir through.

Add the spinach, which will collapse with the heat. Replace the lid and let it cook for a few more minutes until the spinach has wilted.

Serve in a bowl topped with chopped avocado, vegan cheese and vegan sour cream. (Not included in Nutrition Facts)

SLOW COOKER JAMAICAN TOFU & BEAN STEW

SERVES: 4

- 2 packs (approx 280g per pack) cubed hard tofu, drain and squeeze the tofu between your hands
- 2 x 400g can of beans of choice, rinsed and drained
- 3 tablespoons coconut oil
- 1 – 1.3 kg sweet potatoes (cut in large chunks)
- 2-3 large carrots (cut in large chunks)
- 1 small pepper
- 1 medium onion diced
- 2 teaspoons minced ginger
- 2-3 scallions diced
- 1 tablespoon minced garlic
- ¼ teaspoon of dried thyme
- 1 teaspoon allspice
- 1 teaspoon smoked paprika
- 2 bay leaves
- 1 teaspoon hot sauce
- 2 tablespoons tomato paste
- 1 teaspoon vegetable bouillon powder, adjust to taste (optional)
- 2 cups vegetable stock/water or more
- 2-3 tablespoons parsley (optional)
- Salt and pepper to taste

Nutrition Facts

Servings: 4

Amount Per Serving	
Calories 638	
	% Daily Value*
Total Fat 15.7g	20%
Saturated Fat 8.3g	41%
Trans Fat 0g	
Cholesterol 0mg	0%
Sodium 277mg	12%
Potassium 1051mg	22%
Total Carb 88.2g	29%
Dietary Fiber 15.6g	56%
Sugars 49.1g	
Protein 33.9g	
Vitamin A 931%	Vitamin C 61%
Calcium 6%	Iron 17%

*Percent Daily Values are based on a 2,000 calorie diet.

DIRECTIONS

Drain and squeeze the tofu between your hands wrapped in kitchen paper.

Heat the oil a frying pan over medium heat. Add tofu and brown well. Do not overcrowd pan. Cook in batches, if necessary. Add tofu & beans to slow cooker. Then throw in carrots, potatoes, pepper in the slow cooker and salt according to preference.

Add onions, scallions, garlic, thyme, allspice, smoked paprika and bay leaf, hot sauce to the frying pan. Stir for about 2-3 minutes until onions are translucent.

Add tomato paste & bouillon. Stir for another minute, then add water or broth to the pan scrape all sides. Bring to a boil, remove.

Pour in the slow cooker to just cover tofu.

Cover and cook on high for about 3-4 hours or low for 6-7 hours.

SLOW COOKER NEW MEXICO GREEN CHILLI BEAN & TOFU STEW

SERVES: 4

- 2 packs hard tofu, cubed
- 2 tablespoon water
- 6 tablespoon coconut oil
- 1 juice of lime
- 2 tablespoon Mexican seasoning
- 2 x 400g can mixed beans, drained and rinsed
- 3 stalks celery, chopped
- 2 tomatoes, chopped
- 7 green chillies, chopped
- 4 cloves crushed garlic
- 1 litre vegetable stock
- Salt to taste

Nutrition Facts

Servings: 4

Amount Per Serving

Calories 366

	% Daily Value*
Total Fat 22.4g	29%
Saturated Fat 12.6g	63%
Trans Fat 0g	
Cholesterol 0mg	0%
Sodium 288mg	13%
Potassium 662mg	14%
Total Carb 21.4g	7%
Dietary Fiber 7.5g	27%
Sugars 3.7g	
Protein 21.1g	

Vitamin A 17% • Vitamin C 14%
Calcium 21% • Iron 25%

*Percent Daily Values are based on a 2,000 calorie diet.

DIRECTIONS

Can also be made on the hob.

Drain and squeeze the tofu between your hands wrapped in kitchen paper. Mix the water, 3 tablespoons oil, lime juice and the Mexican seasoning in a bowl. Add the tofu and turn to coat on both sides. Marinate for 30 minutes – 1 hour.

In a large frying pan over medium - high heat, brown the tofu in oil, doing so in 2 to 3 batches.

Place the tofu in 3 to 4 litre slow cooker or covered casserole and add beans, celery, tomatoes, chillies and garlic.

Add about 1/4 of the stock to frying pan the tofu was cooked in, stirring over high heat to scrape up browned bits on the bottom and bring to boil. Add to pot with enough additional stock to barely cover the ingredients. Cover and simmer until stew is thick and tofu tender, about 1 1/2 hours on the hob or cook on high for 2¬-3 hours or low for 4¬-6 until tofu is fully cooked. Add salt to taste before serving.

SLOW COOKER TOFU BEAN CASSEROLE

SERVES: 4

- 3 tablespoons coconut oil
- 2 packs (approx. 280g per pack) cubed hard tofu, drain and squeeze the tofu between your hands wrapped in kitchen paper
- ½ small onion, diced
- 3 leeks, washed well and sliced
- 230g mushrooms, halved
- 2 cloves garlic, minced
- 2 tablespoons flour
- 1 tablespoon lemon juice
- 240ml vegetable stock
- 240ml vegan cream
- 400g breadcrumb stuffing mix
- 50g vegan parmesan cheese
- 5 tablespoons dried herbs (rosemary, sage, thyme and parsley or use what you have)
- 1 x 400g cannellini beans
- Salt & pepper to taste

DIRECTIONS

Prepare the night before

Heat coconut oil in large frying pan over medium high heat and add tofu cooking until lightly browned

Remove from pan and set aside. Add onions to the pan and sauté for 2-3 minutes until they start to soften. Add mushroom and leeks and continue to sauté until slightly softened, about 4-5 minutes.

Add minced garlic and sauté for an additional 1-2 minutes. Sprinkle vegetable mix with flour and stir to coat. Slowly stir in lemon juice, stock and then cream and tofu and let simmer for 2-3 minutes. Remove from heat. Stir in stuffing, half of the cheese and herbs. Let cool and place in the fridge.

Morning

Drain and rinse the can of beans, add to tofu mixture and transfer to slow cooker that has been sprayed with non-stick spray. Top with remaining vegan parmesan cheese and cook on high for 2-3 hours or low for 4-6 until tofu is fully cooked. Check seasoning.

Nutrition Facts

Servings: 4

Amount Per Serving

Calories 622

	% Daily Value*
Total Fat 28.8g	37%
Saturated Fat 13.8g	69%
Trans Fat 0g	
Cholesterol 40mg	14%
Sodium 766mg	33%
Potassium 758mg	16%
Total Carb 50.9g	17%
Dietary Fiber 10.4g	37%
Sugars 3.8g	
Protein 40.3g	

Vitamin A 34%	•	Vitamin C 12%
Calcium 74%	•	Iron 33%

*Percent Daily Values are based on a 2,000 calorie diet.

SNACKS

APPLE RINGS

SERVES: 1
- 1 eating apple
- 2 tablespoons of peanut butter

DIRECTIONS

Core the apple and slice into 1cm rings. Top with peanut butter.

It couldn't be simpler!

Nutrition Facts

Servings: 1

Amount Per Serving

Calories 304

	% Daily Value*
Total Fat 16.5g	21%
Saturated Fat 3.4g	17%
Trans Fat 0g	
Cholesterol 0mg	0%
Sodium 149mg	6%
Potassium 446mg	9%
Total Carb 37.1g	12%
Dietary Fiber 7.3g	26%
Sugars 26.2g	
Protein 8.6g	

Vitamin A 0%	Vitamin C 28%
Calcium 0%	Iron 22%

*Percent Daily Values are based on a 2,000 calorie diet.

ULTIMATE PROTEIN FLAPJACKS

SERVES: 12 SLICES

- 170g rolled oats 2 c. *(handwritten: 2+4 c.)*
- 2 scoops vegan protein powder
- 35g desiccated coconut ¼ c.
- 35g whole almonds roughly chopped
- 1 tablespoon chia seeds
- ¼ teaspoon salt
- 110g nut butter ⅓ c.
- 100g agave syrup ⅓ c.
- ½ teaspoon vanilla extract
- ⅛ cup water (or more if needed)

Nutrition

Servings: 12

Amount Per Serving	
Calories 215	
	% Daily Value*
Total Fat 10.2g	13%
Saturated Fat 2.9g	15%
Trans Fat 0g	
Cholesterol 0mg	0%
Sodium 106mg	5%
Potassium 162mg	3%
Total Carb 29.1g	10%
Dietary Fiber 3g	11%
Sugars 2.2g	
Protein 15g	
Vitamin A 1%	Vitamin C 3%
Calcium 4%	Iron 9%

*Percent Daily Values are based on a 2,000 calorie diet.

DIRECTIONS

Line a 9x13 baking pan with wax or parchment paper.

In a large bowl combine the oats, protein powder, coconut, almonds, chia seeds and salt. Mix together.

In a small microwave safe bowl, combine the nut butter and syrup. Microwave for 30 seconds to 1 minute or until the mixture is hot and pourable. Add the vanilla and mix again.

Add the syrup mixture to the dry oat mixture and mix until everything is moist and combined. Press the mixture into the prepared pan and then using the back of a measuring cup press the mixture into the pan until it is tightly packed. Cover and place in the fridge for 1-2 hours. Cut into 12 bars and return to the fridge.

www.thesculptedvegan.com

+ HIGH PROTEIN VEGAN RECIPES

CARROT CAKE GRANOLA BARS

SERVES: 12

- 1 medium carrot, finely grated
- 1 banana, mashed
- 175g rolled oats
- 100g chopped dates
- 30g chopped mix nuts
- 1 teaspoon cinnamon
- Add 2 scoops vanilla or plain protein powder
- Pinch of salt
- 70ml agave or maple syrup
- 70ml melted coconut oil (approx. ¼ cup)
- ¼ teaspoon vanilla extract

DIRECTIONS

Preheat oven to 180°C/350°F/Gas mark 4 and line a 20cm x 20cm baking tin with baking parchment, leaving the parchment to overhang tin.

Combine the carrot, oats, dates, nuts, cinnamon, protein powder, salt, syrup, coconut oil and extract in a large bowl. Mix until fully combined, then spoon into prepared tin. Wet the back of a metal spoon and smooth the mixture.

Cook for 20 – 25 minutes until lightly golden. Remove from oven and leave to cool completely in the tin. Once completely cool, use the overhang parchment paper to remove from the tin. Slice into 12 bars.

Nutrition Facts

Servings: 4

Amount Per Serving	
Calories 171	
	% Daily Value*
Total Fat 8.2g	11%
Saturated Fat 4.9g	24%
Trans Fat 0g	
Cholesterol 0mg	0%
Sodium 18mg	1%
Potassium 141mg	3%
Total Carb 22.9g	8%
Dietary Fiber 3g	11%
Sugars 10.4g	
Protein 13.1g	

Vitamin A 28%	•	Vitamin C 1%
Calcium 2%	•	Iron 6%

*Percent Daily Values are based on a 2,000 calorie diet.

www.thesculptedvegan.com

SNACKS

CHOCOLATE PROTEIN TRUFFLES

SERVES: 10

- 12 dates, pits removed and soaked in water for 4-8 hours
- 1 cup walnuts (lightly toasted if you prefer)
- 2 scoops chocolate protein powder
- 1 tablespoon cold-pressed coconut oil
- ¼ cup unsweetened shredded coconut, plus another ¼ cup for coating
- ½ teaspoon pure vanilla extract
- ½ teaspoon walnut extract
- ½ teaspoon cinnamon
- ½ teaspoon celtic sea salt

DIRECTIONS

Add all the ingredients to either a food processor or the tall cup of a Nutribullet. Pulse until the dates form a thick paste with the nuts evenly distributed throughout. You may need to stop and push the mixture down between pulses.

Add the reserved coconut to a small bowl. Using a teaspoon, form small balls of the paste by rolling in your damp palms (keep a small bowl of water nearby) and roll in the coconut to finish. Arrange the truffles between layers of baking paper in an airtight container and store in the fridge.

Nutrition Facts

Servings: 10

Amount Per Serving	
Calories 142	
	% Daily Value*
Total Fat 10.7g	14%
Saturated Fat 3.2g	16%
Trans Fat 0g	
Cholesterol 0mg	0%
Sodium 174mg	8%
Potassium 164mg	3%
Total Carb 10.5g	4%
Dietary Fiber 2.8g	10%
Sugars 6.7g	
Protein 13.9g	

Vitamin A 0%	•	Vitamin C 0%
Calcium 1%	•	Iron 5%

*Percent Daily Values are based on a 2,000 calorie diet.

www.thesculptedvegan.com

MANGO, LIME & COCONUT FROZEN YOGHURT

SERVES: 2

- 150 g chopped frozen mango
- 125 mls coconut yoghurt / plain vegan yoghurt
- 1 lime
- 2 tablespoons desiccated coconut

DIRECTIONS

Add the desiccated coconut to a pan over a high heat and toast while stirring constantly until golden brown. Set aside.

Zest the lime and set aside the zest. Juice the lime and add to a blender or food processor.

Add the frozen mango and yoghurt to the blender or processor and blitz, stopping to scrape the sides as needed, until smooth, thick and creamy.

Serve immediately topped with the lime zest and toasted coconut

Nutrition Facts

Servings: 2

Amount Per Serving

Calories 248

	% Daily Value*
Total Fat 12.4g	16%
Saturated Fat 10.7g	54%
Trans Fat 0g	
Cholesterol 0mg	0%
Sodium 25mg	1%
Potassium 146mg	3%
Total Carb 35.2g	12%
Dietary Fiber 6.4g	23%
Sugars 25.7g	
Protein 5g	

| Vitamin A 56% | • | Vitamin C 125% |
| Calcium 4% | • | Iron 4% |

*Percent Daily Values are based on a 2,000 calorie diet.

SNACKS

STRAWBERRY PARFAIT

SERVES: 1
- ½ ripe frozen banana chopped
- 100g frozen strawberries
- 60ml plant milk
- 100g coconut yoghurt
- Chopped nuts to top

DIRECTIONS

Blend together the banana, strawberries and milk until smooth.

In a glass tumbler, layer the strawberry mix, and the coconut yoghurt, top with nuts.

Nutrition Facts

Servings: 1

Amount Per Serving

Calories 226

	% Daily Value*
Total Fat 5.3g	7%
Saturated Fat 2.7g	14%
Trans Fat 0g	
Cholesterol 0mg	0%
Sodium 74mg	3%
Potassium 284mg	6%
Total Carb 38.3g	13%
Dietary Fiber 4g	14%
Sugars 27.5g	
Protein 7.9g	

Vitamin A 1%	•	Vitamin C 68%
Calcium 15%	•	Iron 6%

*Percent Daily Values are based on a 2,000 calorie diet.

SOUPS

BLENDED BROCCOLI SOUP

SERVES: 4

- 1 tablespoon coconut oil
- 3/4 medium spring onions, finely sliced
- 2 cloves garlic, crushed
- large head of fresh broccoli, coarsely chopped (including stalk)
- 2 large handfuls of spinach
- 1 tablespoon dried basil
- 1 litre vegetable stock
- 2 cups of almond milk
- 1 tsp sea salt
- A couple of dashes of hot sauce (optional)

Nutrition Facts

Servings: 4

Amount Per Serving

Calories 113

	% Daily Value*
Total Fat 4.9g	6%
Saturated Fat 3g	15%
Trans Fat 0g	
Cholesterol 0mg	0%
Sodium 585mg	25%
Potassium 696mg	15%
Total Carb 14.5g	5%
Dietary Fiber 5.9g	21%
Sugars 4.5g	
Protein 6.3g	

Vitamin A 112% • Vitamin C 243%
Calcium 17% • Iron 12%

*Percent Daily Values are based on a 2,000 calorie diet.

DIRECTIONS

In a large pan heat the oil and sauté the onions and garlic for 1-2 minutes. Stir in the broccoli and salt and sauté until bright green in colour, then cover and cook over a medium heat for 5 minutes. Add the spinach and basil and re-cover for another 5 minutes. Transfer to a food processor or blender with one cup of stock and blend until smooth. Return to the pan and add the remaining stock and the almond milk.

Serve with a couple of dashes of hot sauce.

CURRIED RED LENTIL SOUP

SERVES: 6

- 1 tablespoon coconut oil
- 1 large onion, chopped
- 3 cloves garlic, minced
- 2 tablespoons minced fresh ginger
- 1 jalapeño pepper, seeded and minced (optional)
- 1½ tablespoons curry powder
- 1 teaspoons cinnamon
- 1 teaspoon ground cumin
- 2 bay leaves
- 340g red lentils, rinsed and picked over
- 2ltrs vegetable stock
- 3 tablespoons chopped fresh coriander leaves or parsley
- 2 tablespoons lemon juice
- 2 tablespoons mango chutney
- Salt & freshly ground pepper, to taste
- 80ml plain coconut yoghurt

Nutrition Facts

Servings: 6

Amount Per Serving	
Calories 300	
	% Daily Value*
Total Fat 5.6g	7%
Saturated Fat 3.3g	16%
Trans Fat 0g	
Cholesterol 0mg	0%
Sodium 121mg	5%
Potassium 720mg	15%
Total Carb 47.5g	16%
Dietary Fiber 20.4g	73%
Sugars 6.6g	
Protein 16.9g	
Vitamin A 7%	Vitamin C 16%
Calcium 8%	Iron 37%

*Percent Daily Values are based on a 2,000 calorie diet.

DIRECTIONS

Heat oil in a large saucepan over medium heat. Add onion and cook, stirring occasionally, until softened, 3 to 5 minutes. Add garlic, ginger, jalapeno, curry powder, cinnamon, cumin and bay leaves and cook, stirring often, for about 5 minutes more.

Stir in lentils and stock and bring to a boil. Reduce heat to low and simmer, partially covered, until the lentils are tender, about 45 minutes.

Discard bay leaves. Stir in coriander leaves (or parsley) and lemon juice. Season with pepper. Ladle the soup into bowls and garnish with yoghurt and chutney (if using).

MINESTRONE SOUP

SERVES: 6

- 200g cooked cannellini beans
- 1 bay leaf
- 1 large fresh tomato, chopped
- 1 small sweet potato, peeled
- 1 tablespoon coconut oil
- 2 small red onions, peeled and finely chopped
- 2 carrots, peeled and chopped
- ½ head fennel, chopped
- 3 cloves garlic, peeled and finely sliced
- 1 small bunch fresh basil, leaves and stalks separated
- 800g tinned plum tomatoes
- 2 small courgettes, quartered and sliced
- 200g kale, roughly sliced
- 600ml vegetable stock
- 55g dry quinoa
- Grated vegan cheese to serve (optional)

Nutrition Facts

Servings: 6

Amount Per Serving

Calories 267

	% Daily Value*
Total Fat 3.8g	5%
Saturated Fat 0.5g	2%
Trans Fat 0g	
Cholesterol 0mg	0%
Sodium 125mg	5%
Potassium 1365mg	29%
Total Carb 48g	16%
Dietary Fiber 14.2g	51%
Sugars 10.9g	
Protein 14g	

Vitamin A 326%	•	Vitamin C 154%
Calcium 11%	•	Iron 29%

*Percent Daily Values are based on a 2,000 calorie diet.

DIRECTIONS

Add water to a pan with the potatoes, bay leaf, chopped tomato and season with salt. Cook for 20 minutes then add the beans. Drain the vegetables, reserving the cooking water for later. Heat coconut oil in a pan and add the chopped onions, carrots, fennel, garlic and basil stalks. Season well with salt and pepper and sweat very slowly on a low heat with the lid on for around 15-20 minutes until soft. Add the tomatoes and courgettes and simmer for another 15 mins.

Add the kale, stock, beans and quinoa and stir well. Simmer for around 15 mins or until the quinoa is cooked. If the soup is too thick, add more stock or reserved cooking water. Taste, adjust seasoning and serve sprinkled with the torn-up basil, a drizzle of olive oil and some grated vegan cheese if using. Et voila!

SUPER GREENS & BEAN SOUP

SERVES: 6

- 1 tablespoon coconut oil
- 1 large onion chopped
- 2 garlic cloves chopped
- 6-8 mixed kale & swiss chard leaves stems removed and chopped
- 1 litre low-salt vegetable stock
- 1 x 400g can diced tomatoes
- 2 x 400g cans black beans (if using canned, drain and rinse)
- 1 teaspoon dried oregano
- 2 teaspoons dried basil
- 1/2 teaspoon onion salt
- 4 tablespoons chopped fresh parsley
- 1/4 teaspoon crushed red chilli flakes
- 1/2 teaspoon sea salt
- 1 teaspoon lemon juice

Nutrition Facts

Servings: 6

Amount Per Serving

Calories 343

	% Daily Value*
Total Fat 3.7g	5%
Saturated Fat 2.3g	11%
Trans Fat 0g	
Cholesterol 0mg	0%
Sodium 1189mg	52%
Potassium 1442mg	31%
Total Carb 61.6g	21%
Dietary Fiber 14.8g	53%
Sugars 8.5g	
Protein 19.3g	

Vitamin A 144% • Vitamin C 56%
Calcium 12% • Iron 30%

*Percent Daily Values are based on a 2,000 calorie diet.

DIRECTIONS

In a large pot, on medium heat, sauté the onions and garlic in the oil. Once the onions are translucent, add the remaining ingredients, except for the lemon juice, in the pot. Bring to a boil, then turn down, cover and simmer for about 30 minutes. Lastly add the lemon juice, stir and season to your taste. This can be frozen as well.

Made in the USA
Middletown, DE
24 June 2018